Keto Air Fryer Cookbook for Beginners

Quick & Easy Keto Air Fryer Recipes to Lose Weight and Live Healthy

Jose White

Copyright © 2020 Jose White

All rights reserved. No part of this publication may be reproduced, distributed, or transmitted in any form or by any means, including photocopying, recording, or other electronic or mechanical methods, without the prior written permission of the publisher, except in the case of brief quotations embodied in critical reviews and certain other noncommercial uses permitted by copyright law.

Limit of Liability/Disclaimer of Warranty

While the publisher and author have used their best efforts in preparing this book, they make no representations or warranties with respect to the accuracy or completeness of the contents of this book and specifically disclaim any implied warranties of merchantability or fitness for a particular purpose. No warranty may be created or extended by sales representatives or written sales materials. The advice and strategies contained herein may not be suitable for your situation. You should consult with a professional where appropriate. Neither the publisher nor author shall be liable for any loss of profit or any other commercial damages, including but not limited to special, incidental, consequential, or other damages.

The photography/images contained in this book are properties of Qara Press

ISBN-13: 979- 8645886011

DEDICATION

To all who desire to live life to the fullest!

TABLE OF CONTENT

BASICS OF THE KETOGENIC DIET 1
    Types of Ketogenic diet 2
    Benefits of the Ketogenic Diet 3
    The Ketogenic Diet Food Guide 4

OVERVIEW OF THE AIRFRYER APPLIANCE 7
    Benefits of using an Air Fryer 8

BREAKFAST RECIPES 9
    Beef Tacos 9
    Easy, Air Fryer Buffalo Cauliflower 11
    Cheesy Mushroom Stake 12
    Spicy Scotch Eggs 13
    Air Fried Broccoli Florets 14
    Air Fried Ratatouille 15
    Fried Buffalo Sauced Cauliflower 17
    Simple Air Fryer Lasagna 18
    Bacon Wrapped Jalapeno Chicken 20

CHICKEN & TURKEY RECIPES 23
    Simple Fryer Chicken Breast 23
    Baked Chicken Nuggets 25
    Simple Chicken Tenders 27
    Lemon Cilantro Chicken Wings 28
    Crispy Buffalo Sauce Chicken 30
    Fried Rotisserie Chicken 31

Garlic, Lime Chicken Breast ... 33

Air Fryer Chicken Kebabs ... 34

Fryer Baked Chicken Nuggets ... 35

Chicken Thighs Shish ... 38

Juicy Tandoori Chicken ... 39

Gochujang Glazed Chicken Thighs ... 41

Fryer Cornish Game Hen ... 43

Spicy Indiana Fryer Chicken ... 44

Fryer Chicken Jalafrenzi ... 46

Simple Fryer Chicken Drumsticks ... 47

Pecan Fried Chicken Tenders ... 48

Simple Fryer Turkey Breast ... 49

Peppercorns Marinated Drumsticks ... 51

Baking Powder Fried Chicken Drumettes ... 52

Brown Crust Tenderloins ... 53

Cheesy Pesto Chicken Thighs ... 55

Peanut Garnished Chicken Breast ... 56

BEEF, LAMB & PORK RECIPES ... 59

Simple Pork Chops ... 59

Air *Fried Herbal Pork* Chops ... 60

Simple Lamb Steaks ... 61

Simple Air Fryer Steak ... 63

Simple Bacon Slices Fry ... 64

Air Fried Meatloaves Slide ... 65

Fried Beef Steak Nuggets ... 67

Egg & Bacon Slicone Cups ... 69

Simple Fryer Bacon Slices 70

Ground Kheema Meat Loaf 71

Creamy Taco Seasoned Meatballs 72

Sirloin Steak Bulgogi 73

Bun Thit Nuong 75

Easy, Air Fryer Italian Herb Pork Loin 76

Juicy BBY Baby Ribs 78

German Fryer Rouladen 79

Spicy Fryer Bacon Pieces 81

SEAFOOD RECIPES **83**

Fried Cheese Shrimp 83

Juicy Shrimp Scampi 84

Vegetable Glazed Salmon Fillets 85

Miso Coated Fryer Fillets 87

Air Fried Creamy Scallops 88

Simple Delicious Fryer Fillets 90

Vegetable Salmon Cakes 91

VEGETABLE RECIPES **95**

Fryer Roasted Asian Broccoli Florets 95

Herbal Brussels Sprouts 97

Cauliflower Potato Patties 98

Tofu Fried Cauliflower Rice 100

Cheese Filled Mushrooms 102

Parmesan Cheese Kale Chip 103

Lime Drizzled Asparagus 104

Crispy Vinegar Onion Sprouts 105

Cheesy Cream Spinach 106

Air Fried Pearl Onions 107

Green Beans & Bacon Slices 108

Air Fried Vegetables 109

DESSERTS & APPETIZERS RECIPES 111

Creamy Bacon Stuffed Jalapeno 111

Simple Cream Cheesecake 112

Cheese Filled Jalapeno Poppers 113

Bulgogi Hamburgers 115

Montreal Beef Burgers 117

Simple Air Fryer Hard Boiled Eggs 118

Quick Fryer Sausage 119

Creamy Cheese Queso Fundido 120

Coconut Chicken Meatballs 121

Simple BBQ Meatballs 122

BASICS OF THE KETOGENIC DIET

The ketogenic diet, is a diet with low content of carbohydrate, high fat and a moderate portion of protein.

It's focused on reducing carbohydrate intake, replacing it with fat, thereby leaving the body with the only option of fat as the primary production ingredient for energy.

This process in turn leads to the increased break down of fat in the body, reduction in insulin level, blood sugar and many other health benefits.

Types of Ketogenic diet

There are three types of ketogenic diet, each depending on the dieter and expected result from the diet.

Below are the three versions of ketogenic diet available.

Standard Ketogenic Diet; this is the regular and most popular, with low carbohydrate, high fat and moderate protein. It usually contains 75% fat, 20% protein and 5% carbs.

Cyclical Ketogenic Diet; this type of ketogenic diet allows for a period of higher intake of carbohydrate, for instance, 5 days of the standard ketogenic diet with 2 days of high carbohydrate intake.

Targeted Ketogenic Diet; this type is usually employed by athletes and body builders; it allows them to add extra carbohydrates around their work out routines.

Benefits of the Ketogenic Diet

The ketogenic diet offers its dieters health benefits, from rapid weight loss record, to effective heart disease management and improved mental alertness, these are some of the reasons why the Ketogenic diet has been highly recommended by top medical practitioners for the past few years.

Below is an overview of some of the many benefits of the ketogenic diet.

Drastic Weight Loss

This is one of the most popular benefits of the ketogenic diet known to many people. With ketogenic been a fat burning mechanism, it remains one of the most effective weight loss methods, with dieters experiencing the effect in their body system as early as two weeks into the diet.

Controlled Appetite

The ideology most people have about dieting has to do with starving the body from food which shouldn't be the case as it is not with the ketogenic diet. Unlike many other diet, a ketoer actually enjoys a longer sustainability period, with fat which is naturally sustaining, the desire to eat every time is curbed leading to a controlled appetite.

Controlled Blood Sugar

Most people suffer from diabetes due to the body's inability to control the insulin been produced and with the breakdown of carbohydrate and production of glucose eliminated, insulin is no longer readily needed in the body system which will lead to fewer production, hence a more controlled blood sugar level.

Increase in High-Density Lipoprotein

One of the best ways to increase high-density lipoprotein; often referred to as the good cholesterol, is to eat fat. The higher the level of HDL in the body, the lower the risk of having a heart disease. This is one of the main reasons why the keto diet is recommended to patients to combat heart related diseases.

Mental Alertness

Fats are naturally more sustainable energy givers than carbohydrate and with fat been the fuel behind the body's new energy, the brain can expect an increased supply of energy for its sustenance which in turn leads to more effective performance and extended alertness.

Cholesterol & Blood Pressure Control

Due to a decrease of toxic buildup in the arteries, the blood is able to flow throughout the body as it should without any obstructions and an increase in HDL (the good cholesterol) and decrease in LDL (the bad cholesterol) is experienced.

The Ketogenic Diet Food Guide

The ketogenic diet is not a meal restricting diet, rather it replaces unhealthy meals with health beneficial ones and thus not all foods are advisable for consumption while on the ketogenic diet.

Below is a comprehensive list of the food to avoid and those to take while on the ketogenic diet.

Foods to Consider

Poultry; turkey and chicken

Eggs; organic, pastured and whole

Full-fat dairy; cream, butter and yogurt

Fatty fish; herring, wild-caught salmon and mackerel

Nut butter; almond, natural peanut and cashew butters

Meat; venison, organ meats, pork, bison and grass-fed beef

Condiments: pepper, salt, lemon juice, vinegar, spices and fresh herbs

Non-starchy vegetables; broccoli, greens, mushrooms, tomatoes and peppers

Full-fat cheese; mozzarella, cheddar, goat cheese, brie, and cream cheese

Healthy fats; olive oil, coconut oil, coconut butter, avocado oil, and sesame oil

Nuts & seeds; almonds, macadamia nuts, walnuts, peanuts pumpkin seeds and flaxseeds

Foods to Avoid

Pasta; noodles and spaghetti

Alcoholic beverages: Beer and sugary drinks.

Fruit; grapes, citrus, pineapple and bananas

Grains & grain products; rice, wheat, cereals, oats and tortillas

Beans & legumes; chickpeas, black beans, kidney beans and lentils

Sweetened beverages; juice, soda, sports drinks and sweetened teas

High-carb sauces; dipping sauces, sugary salad dressings and barbecue sauce

Starchy vegetables; sweet potatoes, corn, butternut squash, pumpkin and peas

Sweets & sugary foods; ice cream, sugar, maple syrup, candy, coconut sugar and agave syrup

Bread & baked products; whole-wheat bread, white bread, cookies, crackers, rolls and doughnuts

Keto Friendly Drinks

Sparkling water

Unsweetened coffee

Unsweetened green tea

OVERVIEW OF THE AIRFRYER APPLIANCE

Fried foods are absolutely delicious but, this fries often come with high content of salt, calories and oil which are not the best option for your health. This is why the air fryer offers a better and healthier way to get crispy and tasty feel you really crave.

With an appliance that does not require oil or butter but still provides a deep fry texture, the air fryer helps you to achieve a homemade crispy and crunch that is usually served at fast food stores.

The air fryer simply forces hot air down and around the food, circulating it at a fast rate up to about 400°F.

Benefits of using an Air Fryer

1. Easy & safe to use

2. Your food is prepared faster

3. Decreased amount of calorie content

4. Enjoy healthier food

5. Enjoy crispy, crunchy and tastier meals

6. Help reduce consumption of processed food

7. Little cleaning required

BREAKFAST RECIPES

Beef Tacos

Preparation Time: 10 minutes

Cook Time: 10 minutes

Servings: 6

Ingredients

for the marinade

1/2 teaspoon kosher salt

1 cup diced onion

1 tablespoon soy sauce

1 1/2 pounds diced sirloin beef

2 teaspoons sugar

2 tablespoons gochujang

2 tablespoons sesame oil

2 teaspoons minced garlic

2 teaspoons minced ginger

2 tablespoons sesame seeds

to serve

1/4 cup chopped cilantro, if desired

1/2 cup kimchi, if desired

1/2 cup chopped green scallions

12 flour tortillas

Instructions

1. Add the green onions, diced onions and diced beef into a Ziploc bag.

2. Add in the sesame seeds, sesame oil, sugar, garlic, ginger, soy sauce gochujang and massage into the diced beef.

3. Set the ziploc bag aside to marinate for an hour.

4. Transfer the meat and veggies into the fryer basket then air fry for 12 minutes at 400°F.

5. Serve the vegetable beef on the tortillas leaves then top with the kimchi, cilantro, onions and enjoy as desired.

Nutrition Information

Calories: 241kcal | Carbohydrates: 11g | Protein: 27g | Fat: 10g

Easy, Air Fryer Buffalo Cauliflower

Preparation Time: 5 minutes

Cook Time: 15 minutes

Servings: 4

Ingredients

1/2 cup buffalo sauce

1 tablespoon melted butter

1 cauliflower head, chopped into bites

salt & pepper, to taste

nonstick cooking oil spray

Instructions

1. Combine the sauce, salt, pepper and melted butter together in a small mixing bowl,

2. Spray the fryer basket with the cooking oil spray then add in the cauliflower bites.

3. Air fry at 400°F for 7 minutes then drizzle the cauliflower with the butter mixture and mix until coated.

4. Air fry until the cauliflower turn crisp for an extra 8 minutes.

5. Serve hot and enjoy as desired.

Nutrition Information

Calories: 92kcal | Carbohydrates: 7.3g | Protein: 2.8g | Fat: 6.2g

Cheesy Mushroom Stake

Preparation Time: 10 minutes

Cook Time: 15 minutes

Servings: 4

Ingredients

1/4 cup cream

1/2 teaspoon red pepper flakes

1/2 cup shredded parmesan cheese

1 pack of pasta

1 cup diced onions

1 teaspoon dried thyme

2 teaspoons minced garlic

4 cups mushrooms, sliced

8 ounces shredded mascarpone cheese

kosher salt & black pepper, to taste

Instructions

1. Using a medium sized mixing bowl, add in the pepper flakes, pepper, salt, cream, thyme, cheeses, garlic, onion, mushrooms and combine together.

2. Grease the fryer basket with oil then pour in the mushroom mixture.

3. Air fry the mushroom mix for 15 minutes at 350°F, toss and stir the mixture halfway through.

4. In the meantime, prepare the pasta according to the packet instructions.

5. Serve the cooked pasta into 4 serving bowls then top with even amount of the fried mushroom stake.

6. Garnish the top with the parmesan cheese then serve and enjoy as desired.

Nutrition Information

Calories: 402kcal | Carbohydrates: 10g | Protein: 12g | Fat: 35g

Spicy Scotch Eggs

Preparation Time: 20 minutes

Cook Time: 25 minutes

Servings: 4

Ingredients

1/8 teaspoon ground nutmeg

1-pound pork sausage

1 tablespoon chopped chives

1 cup shaved Parmesan cheese

2 teaspoons ground mustard

2 tablespoons chopped parsley

4 boiled & peeled eggs

kosher salt & black pepper

Instructions

1. Using a large mixing bowl, add in the pepper, salt, nutmeg, parsley, chives, mustard and sausage then combine together.

2. Mold the mixture into 4 patties then add the eggs into each of the patties and mold the patties around the egg.

3. Run the molded patties through the parmesan cheese then transfer into a slightly coated fryer basket.

4. Air fry the patties for 8 minutes at 400°F then flip the patties over and fry for an extra 7 minutes.

5. Serve along with the ground mustard and enjoy as desired.

Nutrition Information

Calories: 533kcal | Carbohydrates: 2g | Protein: 33g | Fat: 43g

Air Fried Broccoli Florets

Preparation Time: 5 minutes

Cook Time: 10 minutes

Servings: 4

Ingredients

1 teaspoon Herbes de Provence

4 cups broccoli florets

salt & pepper, to taste

nonstick cooking oil spray

Instructions

1. Coat the broccoli florets with the cooking oil spray then sprinkle with the seasonings.

2. Coat the fryer basket with the spray then pour in the broccoli florets.

3. Air fry the florets at 360°F for 8 minutes, checking for doneness frequently.

4. Serve hot and enjoy as desired.

Nutrition Information

Calories: 19kcal | Carbohydrates: 1.2g | Protein: 1.7g | Fat: 0.4g

Air Fried Ratatouille

Preparation Time: 15 minutes

Cook Time: 35 minutes

Servings: 2

Ingredients

1/2 teaspoon dried thyme

1 cup cherry tomatoes

1 teaspoon dried oregano

1 cup diced sweet bell peppers

2 cups peeled & cubed eggplant

3 tablespoons coconut oil

7 vertically halved garlic cloves

kosher salt & black pepper

Instructions

1. Using a large mixing bowl, add in the thyme, pepper, salt, oregano, oil, garlic, tomatoes, pepper, eggplant and toss everything together.

2. Transfer the vegetable mixture into the fryer basket then air fry for 20 minutes at 400°F.

3. Serve and enjoy as desired.

Nutrition Information

Calories: 238kcal | Carbohydrates: 12g | Protein: 2g | Fat: 21g

Fried Buffalo Sauced Cauliflower

Preparation Time: 5 minutes

Cook Time: 15 minutes

Servings: 4

Ingredients

1/2 cup buffalo sauce

1 tablespoon melted butter

1 chopped cauliflower head

olive oil, to taste

salt & pepper, to taste

Instructions

1. Generously coat the fryer basket with the oil then set aside.

2. Using a medium sized bowl, add in the buffalo sauce, melted butter, pepper, salt and combine together.

3. Place and arrange the cauliflower bites into the fryer basket then coat with extra oil then fry at 400°F for 7 minutes

4. Open the air fryer up then coat the bites with the sauce mixture then stir around.

5. Fry for an extra 7 minutes until the cauliflower bites turn crisp at 400°F

6. Serve the bites hot and enjoy as desired.

Nutrition Information

Calories: 122kcal | Carbohydrates: 7.3g | Protein: 2.8g | Fat: 9.7g

Simple Air Fryer Lasagna

Preparation Time: 15 minutes

Cook Time: 30 minutes

Servings: 4

Ingredients

for the zucchini

1 sliced zucchini

1 cup marinara sauce

for the sausage

1/2 pound Italian sausage

1 teaspoon minced garlic

1 cup chopped yellow onion

for the cheese mixture

1/2 cup ricotta cheese

1/2 teaspoon minced garlic

1/2 teaspoon Italian Seasoning

1/2 teaspoon ground black pepper

1/2 cup mozzarella cheese, shredded

1/2 cup divided & shredded parmesan cheese

1 large egg

Instructions

1. Arrange the zucchini in the fryer basket then top with 1/4 cup of the marinara sauce.

2. Using a large mixing bowl, add in the garlic, onions, sausage and incorporate together then layer over the zucchini slices.

3. Pour in the remaining marinara sauce over the meat layer.

4. Using another mixing bowl, add in 1/4 cup parmesan, mozzarella and ricotta cheese, pepper, garlic, seasoning and egg then combine.

5. Pour the cheese mixture on the meat layer then top with the remaining parmesan cheese.

6. Place the basket, covered with aluminum foil into the air fryer and bake for 20 minutes at 350°F.

7. Peel off the aluminum foil then bake for an extra 10 minutes.

8. Allow the lasagna to cool off for a bit then serve and enjoy as desired.

Nutrition Information

Calories: 357kcal | Carbohydrates: 8g | Protein: 17g | Fat: 27g

Bacon Wrapped Jalapeno Chicken

Preparation Time: 15 minutes

Cook Time: 15 minutes

Servings: 4

Ingredients

1/4 cup cream cheese

1/4 cup shredded parmesan cheese

1/2 cup thawed & drained frozen spinach

2 large 1/2" thick chicken breasts

2 tablespoons chopped jalapeño peppers

4 teaspoons cajun seasoning

6 bacon slices

kosher salt & black pepper

Instructions

1. Using a small mixing bowl, add the salt, pepper, jalapenos, cheeses, spinach then combine together.

2. Coat the chicken breasts with the mixture, ensuring every part is covered.

3. Season the chicken with the cajun seasoning then wrap each in even slices of bacon.

4. Transfer the wrapped breast into the fryer basket then air fry for 30 minutes at 350°F.

5. Serve and enjoy as desired.

Nutrition Information

Calories: 357kcal | Carbohydrates: 4g | Protein: 33g | Fat: 23g

CHICKEN & TURKEY RECIPES

Simple Fryer Chicken Breast

Preparation Time: 10 minutes

Cook Time: 50 minutes

Servings: 10

Ingredients

1/8 teaspoon salt

1/3 teaspoon oregano

1/2 teaspoon thyme

1/2 teaspoon basil

1 cup almond milk

1 teaspoon celery salt

1 teaspoon black pepper

1 tablespoon avocado oil

1 teaspoon dried mustard

1 teaspoon ground ginger

1 tablespoon white vinegar

2 teaspoons garlic salt

2 cups pork rinds, crushed

3 teaspoons white pepper

4 teaspoons paprika

5 pounds' chicken breast

Instructions

1. Place the chicken breast in a mixing bowl then set aside and combine the vinegar and almond milk together.

2. Cover the chicken breast with the vinegar mixture then place in the refrigerator to marinate for 2 hours.

3. Using a shallow dish, add in pork rinds, thyme, salt, oregano, basil, black pepper, celery salt, paprika, dried mustard, ground ginger, garlic salt, white pepper and incorporate together.

4. Dredge each piece of the marinated chicken in the pork rinds mixture and coat.

5. Pour the coconut oil into the fryer basket then add in the coated chicken pieces in a single layer.

6. Fry for 10 minutes at 360°F then flip and fry for an extra 10 minutes then check for doneness to taste.

7. Serve and enjoy as desired.

Nutrition Information

Calories: 539kcal | Carbohydrates: 1g | Protein: 45g | Fat: 37g

Baked Chicken Nuggets

Preparation Time: 10 minutes

Cook Time: 15 minutes

Servings: 4

Ingredients

1/4 cup coconut flour

1/2 teaspoon ground ginger

1 teaspoon coconut oil

1 pound chopped chicken thighs, boneless & skinless

4 egg whites

6 tablespoons sesame seeds, toasted

sea salt, to taste

nonstick cooking oil spray

for the sauce

1/2 teaspoon monk fruit

1/2 teaspoon ground ginger

1 tablespoon water

1 teaspoon sriracha

2 teaspoons rice vinegar

2 tablespoons almond butter

4 teaspoons coconut aminos

Instructions

1. Heat the air fryer up for 10 minutes to 400°F

2. In the meantime, toss the chopped chicken with the salt & oil until well coated.

3. Pour the ground ginger and coconut flour into a ziploc bag then add in the chicken pieces and thoroughly shake around.

4. Add the egg whites into a mixing bowl, then add in the coated chicken nuggets and toss until covered with the egg whites.

5. Shake the chicken pieces off of excess egg whites then pour the toasted sesame seeds into the ziploc bag, add the chicken pieces back into the bag and shake again to coat.

6. Grease the fryer basket with the cooking spray oil then add in the coated chicken nuggets and cook for 6 minutes.

7. Flip each chicken piece over after 6 minutes and cook until crispy for an extra 6 minutes.

8. In the meantime, combine all the sauce ingredients together until incorporated then serve alongside the crispy nuggets and enjoy.

Nutrition Information

Calories: 1683kcal | Carbohydrates: 99.1g | Protein: 35g | Fat: 129.1g

Simple Chicken Tenders

Preparation Time: 8 minutes

Cook Time: 10 minutes

Servings: 2

Ingredients

1/2 teaspoon powdered onion

1/2 teaspoon powdered garlic

1 cup almond flour

1 teaspoon paprika

1 teaspoon Italian seasoning

1 1/2 pounds' chicken tenders

2 large eggs

2 tablespoon ground flax seed

nonstick cooking oil spray

sea salt & black pepper, to taste

Instructions

1. Heat the fryer up for 10 minutes to 400°F

2. Break the eggs into a mixing bowl and whisk together then combine the flaxseed, almond flour and remaining seasoning (except the salt & pepper) in a separate bowl until combined.

3. Dry the chicken tenders and season with salt, pepper then dip until coated in the whisked egg and in then the flaxseed mixture.

4. Coat the fryer basket with the cooking oil spray then add the chicken tenders into the basket with enough space in between them.

5. Air fry for 5 minutes then flip the chicken over and fry for an extra 5 minutes.

6. Repeat the same process if there are any uncooked chicken then serve with any sauce of choice and enjoy as desired.

Nutrition Information

Calories 315kcal | Carbohydrate:12.9g | Protein: 17.2g | Fat: 21.1g

Lemon Cilantro Chicken Wings

Preparation Time: 10 minutes

Cook Time: 20 minutes

Servings: 4

Ingredients

1/2 lemon juice

1 teaspoon soy sauce

1 teaspoon avocado oil

1 teaspoon chicken seasoning

2 tablespoons chopped fresh cilantro

4 boneless chicken wings

salt & pepper, to taste

Instructions

1. Combine the soy sauce, lemon juice, avocado oil and generously drizzle over and around the chicken wings.

2. Season with the salt, pepper and chicken seasoning until well coated then transfer into a ziploc bag and add in the cilantro.

3. Transfer the ziploc bag into the freezer and marinate for about an hour.

4. Once marinated, add the chicken wings into the fryer basket then cook at 400°F for 10 minutes.

5. After 10 minutes, flip the chicken wings over and cook until tenderized for an extra 10 minutes.

6. Once done, allow to cool off for a bit then serve and enjoy as desired.

Nutrition Information

Calories: 65kcal | Carbohydrates: 4.5g | Protein: 4.2g | Fat: 3.4g

Crispy Buffalo Sauce Chicken

Preparation Time: 10 minutes

Cook Time: 25 minutes

Servings: 6

Ingredients

1/4 cup buffalo wing sauce

1 teaspoon powdered garlic

2 teaspoons low-salt soy sauce

16 chicken wings drummettes

cooking oil spray

black pepper, to taste

chicken seasoning, to taste

Instructions

1. Drizzle the chicken drummettes with the soy sauce then season with the powdered garlic, pepper and chicken seasoning.

2. Transfer the seasoned chicken into the fryer basket then coat with the cooking oil spray and cook at 400°F for 5 minutes.

3. Shake the basket after 10 minutes then return back into in the air fryer and fry for an extra 5 minutes.

4. Glaze each of the chicken pieces with the buffalo sauce then return into the air fryer and fry until crisp for 10 more minutes.

5. Once done, allow the chicken to cool for a bit then serve and enjoy as desired.

Nutrition Information

Calories: 39kcal | Carbohydrates: 2.7g | Protein: 1.1g | Fat: 2.3g

Fried Rotisserie Chicken

Preparation Time: 15 minutes

Cook Time: 55 minutes

Servings: 5

Ingredients

1/4 diced onion

1/2 fresh lime

1 teaspoon ground thyme

1 teaspoon powdered onion

1 teaspoon powdered garlic

4 fresh thyme sprigs

4 fresh rosemary sprigs

5-pound whole chicken

cooking oil spray

salt & pepper, to taste

Instructions

1. Scoop the contents of the chicken cavity out then stuff in the thyme & rosemary sprigs, diced onion and lime then pat dry the body of the chicken and coat with the cooking oil.

2. Thoroughly season each side of the chicken with the remaining seasoning ingredients.

3. Prepare the fryer basket with parchment paper then add in the season and loaded chicken and air fry at 330°F for 30 minutes.

4. Open the air fryer and flip the chicken over and sprinkle with extra seasoning if required then air fry for another 25 minutes.

5. Check for desired doneness all over the chicken before removing it from the fryer.

6. Allow the chicken to cool off for a bit then dice, serve and enjoy as desired.

Nutrition Information

Calories: 57kcal | Carbohydrates: 3.2g | Protein: 8.7g | Fat: 2.5g

Garlic, Lime Chicken Breast

Preparation Time: 5 minutes

Cook Time: 20 minutes

Servings: 3

Ingredients

1 1/2 pounds' chicken breasts

3 tablespoons garlic & lime marinade

salt & pepper, to taste

chicken seasoning, to taste

Instructions

1. Generously cover the chicken breast in the garlic lime marinade then sprinkle with the salt, pepper & chicken seasoning.

2. Prepare the fryer basket with parchment paper then place in the coated chicken breasts.

3. Air fry at 360°F for 10 minutes then flip the chicken breasts over and cook for an extra 10 minutes.

4. Allow the chicken breast to cool off for a bit then dice as desired, serve and enjoy.

Nutrition Information

Calories: 70kcal | Carbohydrates: 7.1g | Protein: 7.3g | Fat: 1.9g

Air Fryer Chicken Kebabs

Preparation Time: 15 minutes

Cook Time: 20 minutes

Servings: 5

Ingredients

1/4 diced red onion

1/2 diced zucchini

1/2 diced red pepper

1/2 diced green pepper

1/2 diced yellow pepper

1 teaspoon bbq seasoning

1 tablespoon chicken seasoning

2 tablespoons soy sauce

5 grape tomatoes

16 ounces 1" cubed chicken breasts

salt & pepper, to taste

nonstick cooking oil spray

Instructions

1. Pat dry the chicken breasts then combine the bbq seasoning, chicken seasoning, salt, pepper and soy sauce together.

2. Generously coat the chicken cubes with the soy sauce mixture then set aside to marinate for about an hour.

3. Sew the marinated chicken cubes onto the wooden skewers.

4. Alternatively layer the chicken cubes with onions, zucchini, pepper and top each skewer with a grape tomato.

5. Spray the layered skewers with the cooking oil then line the fryer basket with parchment paper and fit in a small grill rack.

6. Place the skewers on the grill rack then air fry at 350°F for 10 minutes.

7. Flip the skewers over and fry for an additional 10 minutes.

8. Allow the chicken to cool for a bit then serve and enjoy with any sauce of choice.

Nutrition Information

Calories: 225kcal | Carbohydrates: 5.4g | Protein: 24.8g | Fat: 12.2g

Fryer Baked Chicken Nuggets

Preparation Time: 10 minutes

Cook Time: 12 minutes

Servings: 4

Ingredients

1/8 teaspoon sea salt

1/4 cup coconut flour

1/2 teaspoon ground ginger

1 teaspoon sesame oil

1-pound chicken breast, boneless & skinless

4 large egg whites

6 tablespoons toasted sesame seeds

nonstick cooking oil spray

for the dip

1/2 teaspoon monk fruit

1/2 teaspoon ground ginger

1 tablespoon water

1 teaspoon sriracha

2 teaspoons rice vinegar

2 tablespoons almond butter

4 teaspoons coconut aminos

Instructions

1. Chop the chicken breast into 1" nuggets then pat dry and place in a medium sized mixing bowl.

2. Pour in the sesame oil, salt and massage into the chicken nuggets.

3. Pour the ground ginger and coconut flour into a large ziploc bag then add in the coated chicken nuggets and shake around to coat.

4. Transfer the chicken nuggets into a bowl filled with the egg whites and toss around until covered in the whites.

5. Shake off excess white from the nuggets then cover with the sesame seeds.

6. Heat the fryer up 400°F for 10 minutes then coat the basket with oil and add in the covered chicken nuggets and fry for 6 minutes.

7. Flip the chicken nuggets over and cook until crispy for 6 extra minutes.

8. In the meantime, combine all the sauce ingredients together until mixed.

9. Serve the fried nuggets along with the sauce and enjoy as desired.

Nutrition Information

Calories: 293kcal | Carbohydrates: 10.4g | Protein: 33.3g | Fat: 13.8g

Chicken Thighs Shish

Preparation Time: 45 minutes

Cook Time: 15 minutes

Servings: 4

Ingredients

1/4 cup full-fat Greek yogurt

1/2 teaspoon cayenne pepper

1/2 teaspoon ground cinnamon

1/2 teaspoon ground black pepper

1 teaspoon kosher salt

1 teaspoon ground cumin

1 tablespoon juiced lime

1 tablespoon avocado oil

1 teaspoon smoked paprika

1 tablespoon tomato paste

1 tablespoon minced garlic

1-pound chicken thighs, boneless & skinless

Instructions

1. Using a large mixing bowl, add in the tomato paste, garlic, oil, juiced lime, cumin, salt, black pepper, cinnamon, paprika, cayenne pepper, yogurt and mix until combined.

2. Add the chicken pieces into the mixing bowl and toss until combined, then set aside to marinate for an hour.

3. Arrange the marinated chicken in the fryer basket then cook for 10 minutes at 370°F.

4. Flip the chicken over and cook for an additional 5 minutes.

5. Serve and enjoy as desired.

Nutrition Information

Calories: 298kcal | Carbohydrates: 4g | Protein: 20g | Fat: 23g

Juicy Tandoori Chicken

Preparation Time: 30 minutes

Cook Time: 15 minutes

Servings: 4

Ingredients

1/4 cup cilantro

1/4 cup Greek yogurt

1/2 teaspoon cayenne pepper

1 teaspoon turmeric

1 teaspoon kosher salt

1 teaspoon garam masala

1 teaspoon smoked paprika

1 tablespoon minced ginger

1 pound halved chicken tenders

1 tablespoon minced garlic cloves

to garnish

1 tablespoon coconut oil

2 teaspoons juiced lime

2 tablespoons chopped cilantro

Instructions

1. Add in all the ingredients (except the one for garnishing) into a mixing bowl then combine and marinate for minutes.

2. Arrange the marinated chicken in the fryer basket then generously baste with the coconut oil.

3. Air fry the chicken for 10 minutes at 350°F then flip the chicken over, baste the other side and cook for an extra 5 minutes.

4. Serve and top with the juiced lime, enjoying with a garnish of cilantro.

Nutrition Information

Calories: 178kcal | Carbohydrates: 2g | Protein: 25g | Fat: 6g

Gochujang Glazed Chicken Thighs

Preparation Time: 10 minutes

Cook Time: 30 minutes

Servings: 4

Ingredients

for the chicken

2 pounds' chicken thighs

kosher salt & black pepper, to taste

for the sauce

1 teaspoon agave nectar

1 tablespoon mayonnaise

1 tablespoon avocado oil

1 tablespoon minced ginger

1 tablespoon minced garlic cloves

2 packets sugar

2 tablespoons gochujang

to garnish

1/4 cup chopped green scallions

2 teaspoons sesame seeds

Instructions

1. Generously season the salt the chicken thighs then air fry for 10 minutes at 400°F.

2. Flip the chicken thighs over then air fry for an additional 10 minutes.

3. In the meantime, combine all the sauce ingredients together then set aside to marinate.

4. Transfer the fried chicken thighs into a mixing bowl, then baste with half of the sauce ingredients.

5. Return the coated chicken into the air fryer then air fry until the sauce is glazed over for an extra 5 minutes.

6. Serve, garnished with the green onions, sesame seeds and enjoy as desired.

Nutrition Information

Calories: 356kcal | Carbohydrates: 6g | Protein: 23g | Fat: 26g

Fryer Cornish Game Hen

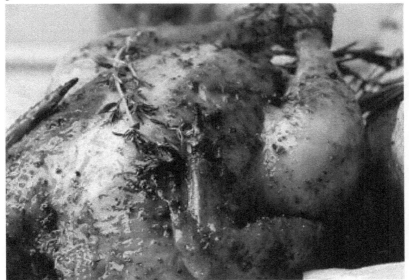

Preparation Time: 45 minutes

Cook Time: 20 minutes

Servings: 4

Ingredients

1/4 cup fish sauce

1 teaspoon turmeric

1 tablespoon soy sauce

1 chopped jalapeño peppers

1 cup chopped cilantro leaves

2 tablespoon stevia

2 teaspoon ground coriander

2 tablespoon lemongrass paste

2 halved whole cornish game hens, with the giblets removed

8 minced garlic cloves

salt & black pepper, to taste

Instructions

1. Using a high speed blender, add in the turmeric, salt, coriander, pepper, lemongrass paste, sugar, garlic, cilantro, fish sauce and incorporate together.

2. Add in the broiler chicken and toss together until fully coated with the mixture then set aside to marinate for an hour.

3. Transfer the marinated broiler into the fryer basket and air fry for 10 minutes at 400°F.

4. Flip the broiler over then cook for an extra 10 minutes.

5. Serve and enjoy as desired.

Nutrition Information

Calories: 222kcal | Carbohydrates: 4g | Protein: 14g | Fat: 9g

Spicy Indiana Fryer Chicken

Preparation Time: 10 minutes

Cook Time: 15 minutes

Servings: 4

Ingredients

for the chicken

1 teaspoon turmeric

1 diced large onion

1 tablespoon avocado oil

1 teaspoons garam masala

1 teaspoons smoked paprika

1 teaspoons ground fennel seeds

1-pound chicken breast, boneless & skinless

2 teaspoons minced ginger

2 teaspoons minced garlic cloves

nonstick cooking oil spray

salt & cayenne pepper, to taste

to top

1/4 cup chopped cilantro

2 teaspoons juiced lime

Instructions

1. Make slight piercing all over the chicken breast then set aside.

2. Using a large mixing bowl add in all the remaining ingredients and combine together.

3. Add the pierced chicken breast into the bowl then set aside for an hour to marinate.

4. Transfer the marinated chicken and veggies into the fryer basket then coat with the cooking oil spray.

5. Cook for 15 minutes at 360°F then serve and enjoy with a garnish of cilantro topped with the juiced lime.

Nutrition Information

Calories: 305kcal | Carbohydrates: 6g | Protein: 19g | Fat: 23g

Fryer Chicken Jalafrenzi

Preparation Time: 10 minutes

Cook Time: 15 minutes

Servings: 4

Ingredients

1 cup diced onions

1 teaspoon turmeric

1 teaspoon garam masala

1 pound skinless & boneless chicken breasts, diced into 2" cubes

2 cups chopped bell peppers

2 tablespoons avocado oil

kosher salt & cayenne pepper, to taste

for the sauce

1/4 cup tomato sauce

1 tablespoon water

1 teaspoon garam masala

kosher salt & cayenne pepper, to taste

Instructions

1. Using a large mixing bowl add in the salt, pepper, garam masala, turmeric, oil, salt, bell pepper, onions, chicken breasts then incorporate together.

2. Pour the mixture into the fryer basket then air fry for 15 minutes at 360°F, stirring the contents halfway through cook time.

3. In the meantime, add all the sauce ingredients into a microwave safe dish then microwave for a minute until blended together.

4. Serve and enjoy the chicken vegetables with the prepared sauce.

Nutrition Information

Calories: 247kcal | Carbohydrates: 9g | Protein: 23g | Fat: 12g

Simple Fryer Chicken Drumsticks

Preparation Time: 10 minutes

Cook Time: 20 minutes

Servings: 2

Ingredients

1/2 cup cilantro, chopped

1/2 jalapeño peppers, chopped

1 teaspoon kosher salt

2 chopped ginger

2 tablespoons juiced lime

2 tablespoons coconut oil

4 chicken drumsticks

8 minced garlic cloves

Instructions

1. Make slight incisions on the chicken drumsticks then add into a ziploc bag.

2. Using a medium mixing bowl, add in the ginger, garlic, pepper, cilantro, oil, salt, juiced lime and incorporate together.

3. Pour the mixture into the drumstick ziploc bag then allow to marinate for 1 hour.

4. Transfer the marinated drumstick into the fryer basket then air fry for 10 minutes at 390°F.

5. Flip the drumsticks over then fry for an extra 10 minutes.

6. Serve and enjoy as desired.

Nutrition Information

Calories: 389kcal | Carbohydrates: 6g | Protein: 28g | Fat: 28g

Pecan Fried Chicken Tenders

Preparation Time: 5 minutes

Cook Time: 12 minutes

Servings: 4

Ingredients

1/4 cup roughly chopped mustard

1/2 teaspoon smoked paprika

1 cup crushed pecans

1-pound chicken tenders

2 tablespoons maple syrup

kosher salt & black pepper

Instructions

1. Add the chicken tenders into a large mixing bowl then add in the paprika, salt, pepper and combine until coated.

2. Pour in the mustard, maple syrup and toss around again then add the crushed pecans into a flat plate.

3. Run each tender through the crushed pecans until covered all over then transfer into the fryer basket.

4. Air fry for 12 minutes at 350°F.

5. Serve and enjoy as desired.

Nutrition Information

Calories: 325kcal | Carbohydrates: 8g | Protein: 27g | Fat: 21g

Simple Fryer Turkey Breast

Preparation Time: 5 minutes

Cook Time: 45 minutes

Servings: 4

Ingredients

1/2 tablespoon poultry seasoning

1 teaspoon sage, dried

1 teaspoon thyme, dried

2 tablespoons coconut oil

4-pound bone-in turkey breast

salt & pepper, to taste

Instructions

1. Generously massage the oil all over the turkey breast then coat with the seasonings.

2. Transfer the coated turkey into the fryer basket then fry at 350°F for 25 minutes.

3. Flip the turkey over then cook for another 20-25 minutes until tenderized and crispy as desired.

4. Allow the turkey to cool for a bit then dice, serve and enjoy.

Nutrition Information

Calories: 86kcal | Carbohydrates: 0.6g | Protein: 4.4g | Fat: 8.1g

Peppercorns Marinated Drumsticks

Preparation Time: 5 minutes

Cook Time: 25 minutes

Servings: 4

Ingredients

1/4 cup juiced lemon

1/2 teaspoon cayenne pepper

1/2 teaspoon coriander seeds

1/2 teaspoon whole black peppercorns

1 teaspoon turmeric

1 teaspoon kosher salt

1 teaspoon cumin seeds

1 teaspoon parsley, dried

1 teaspoon oregano, dried

1 1/2 pounds chicken drumsticks

2 tablespoons coconut oil

Instructions

1. Using a high speed blender, add in the peppercorns, kosher salt, cayenne pepper, coriander seeds, parsley, oregano, cumin, turmeric and blend together until smooth.

2. Transfer the blended spices into a mixing bowl, then add in the oil, juiced lemon and incorporate together.

3. Add in the drumsticks then toss to coat and allow to marinate for an hour.

4. Arrange the drumsticks in the fryer basket with the skin side up and air fry for 15 minutes at 390°F.

5. Flip the chicken drumstick over then fry for an extra 10 minutes.

6. Serve and enjoy as desired.

Nutrition Information

Calories: 253kcal | Carbohydrates: 2g | Protein: 20g | Fat: 17g

Baking Powder Fried Chicken Drumettes

Preparation Time: 5 minutes

Cook Time: 25 minutes

Servings: 4

Ingredients

1 tablespoon baking powder

2 pounds chicken wings drumettes

cooking oil spray

salt & pepper, to taste

chicken seasoning, to taste

Instructions

1. Add the chicken drumetes into a ziploc bag then pour in the pepper, salt, chicken seasoning and massage together.

2. Pour in the baking powder and massage again until coated all over then transfer into the fryer basket and spray with the cooking oil.

3. Air fry at 320°F for 15 minutes then flip the chicken over, spray with extra cooking oil and air fry until crispy to taste for an extra 10 minutes at 400°F.

4. Once done, allow the chicken drumettes to cool off for a bit then serve and enjoy ad desired.

Nutrition Information

Calories: 582kcal | Carbohydrates: 4g | Protein: 44g | Fat: 42.6g

Brown Crust Tenderloins

Preparation Time: 15 minutes

Cook Time: 15 minutes

Servings: 4

Ingredients

1/2 cup almond flour

1/2 teaspoon chili powder

1/2 cup shredded parmesan cheese

1 beaten large eggs

1-pound chicken tenderloins

kosher salt & black pepper, to taste

Instructions

1. Add the chili powder, pepper, salt, shredded cheese and almond flour into a mixing bowl then mix together.

2. Dip the tenderloins into the whisked egg then coat with the flour mixture.

3. Coat the fryer basket with cooking oil then add in the dredged tenderloins.

4. Cook for 12 minutes at 350°F, flipping the tenderloins halfway through cook time.

5. Continue to air fry for 3 more minutes, this time at 400°F to make the crust brown.

6. Serve and enjoy as desired.

Nutrition Information

Calories: 280kcal | Carbohydrates: 4g | Protein: 33g | Fat: 15g

Cheesy Pesto Chicken Thighs

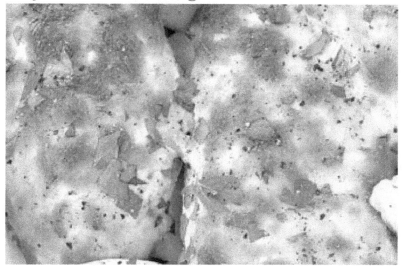

Preparation Time: 10 minutes

Cook Time: 15 minutes

Servings: 4

Ingredients

1/4 cup half & half

1/4 cup sliced bell peppers

1/4 cup diced red bell pepper

1/4 cup parmesan cheese, shredded

1/2 cup pesto

1/2 cup diced onion

1/2 cup halved cherry tomatoes

1 teaspoon red pepper flakes

1 pound halved chicken thighs, boneless & skinless

Instructions

1. Using a medium sized mixing bowl, add in the pepper flakes, parmesan cheese, half & half, pesto and combine together.

2. Add the halved chicken thighs into the mixture then coat and allow to marinate for an hour.

3. Transfer the marinade sauce and chicken halves into the fryer basket then garnish with the tomatoes, pepper and onions.

4. Air fry the chicken sauce for 15 minutes at 360°F.

5. Serve and enjoy as desired.

Nutrition Information

Calories: 432kcal | Carbohydrates: 7g | Protein: 23g | Fat: 34g

Peanut Garnished Chicken Breast

Preparation Time: 15 minutes

Cook Time: 20 minutes

Servings: 4

Ingredients

for the sauce

1/4 cup creamy peanut butter

1/2 cup boiling water

1 tablespoon soy sauce

1-pound chicken breasts

1 teaspoon diced ginger

1 teaspoon minced garlic

1 tablespoon sriracha sauce

2 tablespoons juiced lemon

2 tablespoons sweet thai chili sauce

kosher salt, to taste

to garnish

1/4 cup chopped green scallions

3 tablespoons crushed peanuts

6 teaspoons chopped cilantro

Instructions

1. Using a small mixing bowl add in the salt, juiced lemon, chili sauce, sriracha, soy sauce, peanut butter and whisk together.

2. Pour the boiling water into the mixing bowl and incorporate with the peanut butter mix until smooth.

3. Add the chicken breasts into a ziploc bag then pour in half of the sauce mixture and massage into the chicken breast.

4. Set the ziploc bag aside to marinate for an hour then take out and transfer into the fryer basket.

5. Air fry for 20 minutes at 350°F.

6. Serve, garnished with the crushed peanuts, onion, cilantro and enjoy.

Nutrition Information

Calories: 361kcal | Carbohydrates: 10g | Protein: 22g | Fat: 27g

BEEF, LAMB & PORK RECIPES

Simple Pork Chops

Preparation Time: 15 minutes

Cook Time: 15 minutes

Servings: 4

Ingredients

1/2 cup water

1 teaspoon sugar

4 pork chops

melted butter

kosher salt, to taste

Instructions

1. Combine the water, sugar and salt into a mixing bowl.

2. Add the pork chops into the water mixture and brine.

3. Pat dry the pork chops then coat with the melted butter.

4. Place the coated chops into the fryer basket then air fry for 15 minutes at 380°F.

5. Once done, serve and enjoy as desired.

Nutrition Information

Calories: 208kcal | Protein: 29g | Fat: 9g

Air Fried Herbal Pork Chops

Preparation Time: 10 minutes

Cook Time: 15 minutes

Servings: 2

Ingredients

1/2 teaspoon red pepper flakes

1 lime zest

1 teaspoon chopped fresh sage

1 teaspoon chopped fennel seeds

1 tablespoon coconut oil, with extra

2 minced garlic cloves

2 tablespoons avocado oil

2 teaspoons chopped fresh rosemary

2 (8 ounces) center cut (1" thick) pork chops

kosher salt & ground pepper

Instructions

1. Using a medium mixing bowl, add in a tablespoon avocado oil, lime zest, salt, garlic, pepper, sage, red pepper, fennel seeds and rosemary.

2. Toss the ingredients together until combined, crushing the herbs with the back of the spoon.

3. Generously coat the pork chop with the rosemary mixture then transfer into the fryer basket.

4. Air fry for 15 minutes at 380°F, flipping the pork chops over halfway through cook time.

5. Serve and enjoy as desired.

Nutrition Information

Calories: 203kcal | Carbohydrates: 4g | Protein: 1g | Fat: 21g

Simple Lamb Steaks

Preparation Time: 40 minutes

Cook Time: 15 minutes

Servings: 4

Ingredients

1/2 diced onion

1/2 teaspoon ground cardamom

1 teaspoon garam masala

1 teaspoon ground fennel

1 teaspoon ground cinnamon

1-pound lamb sirloin steaks, boneless

4 chopped ginger

5 minced garlic cloves

kosher salt & cayenne pepper, to taste

Instructions

1. Using a high speed blender, add in all the ingredients (except the lamb steaks) and pulse until blended.

2. Make small incisions on the body of the lamb steaks then place into a large ziploc bag.

3. Pour the blender marinade into the ziploc bag and allow the steaks to marinate for an hour.

4. Transfer the marinated steaks into the fry basket and air fry for 8 minutes at 330°F.

5. Flip the lamb steaks over thin air fry for another 7 minutes.

6. Serve hot and enjoy as desired.

Nutrition Information

Calories: 182kcal | Carbohydrates: 3g | Protein: 24g | Fat: 7g

Simple Air Fryer Steak

Preparation Time: 5 minutes

Cook Time: 10 minutes

Servings: 2

Ingredients

1/2 tablespoon powdered cocoa, unsweetened

1 tablespoon steak rub

1 teaspoon liquid smoke

1 tablespoon low-salt soy sauce

8 ounces steaks

melted butter

salt & pepper, to taste

Instructions

1. Drizzle the steaks with the liquid smoke, soy sauce and massage until incorporated then season with the steak rub.

2. Transfer the seasoned steak into the refrigerator to marinate for 2 hours.

3. Once marinated, place the steak in the fryer basket then fry at 370°F for 5 minutes.

4. Check the steak for desired doneness then cook for extra minutes if desired until tender and crispy to taste.

5. Serve, drizzled with the melted butter and enjoy as desired.

Nutrition Information

Calories: 183kcal | Carbohydrates: 1.6g | Protein: 21.7g | Fat: 9.6g

Simple Bacon Slices Fry

Preparation Time: 4 minutes

Cook Time: 11 minutes

Servings: 10

Ingredients

10 bacon slices

beef seasoning

Instructions

1. Generously coat the bacon slices with the seasonings.

2. Place the seasoned slices into the fryer basket.

3. Cook for 10 minutes at 400°F until crispy to taste.

4. Serve and enjoy as desired.

Nutrition Information

Calories: 91kcal | Protein: 2g | Fat: 8g

Air Fried Meatloaves Slide

Preparation Time: 10 minutes

Cook Time: 10 minutes

Servings: 10

Ingredients

1/4 cup ketchup

1/4 cup diced onion

1/4 cup coconut flour

1/2 teaspoon sea salt

1/2 teaspoon black pepper

1/2 teaspoon dried tarragon

1/2 cup blanched almond flour

1-pound ground beef

1 minced garlic clove

1 teaspoon Italian seasoning

1 tablespoon Worcestershire sauce

2 beaten eggs

Instructions

1. Using a large mixing bowl, add in all ingredients and incorporate together until a batter is formed.

2. Mold 10 even loaves from the patties then transfer into the refrigerator to firm up for about 15 minutes.

3. Transfer the firm loaves into the fryer basket and air fry at 360°F for 10 minutes.

4. If cooking in batches, keep the cooked ones warm until done cooking.

5. Serve hot and enjoy as desired.

Nutrition Information

Calories: 228kcal | Carbohydrates: 6g | Protein: 13g | Fat: 5g

Fried Beef Steak Nuggets

Preparation Time: 10 minutes

Cook Time: 5 minutes

Servings: 4

Ingredients

1 large egg

1 pound diced beef steak

coconut oil for frying

for the breading

1/2 cup pork panko

1/2 teaspoon seasoned salt

1/2 cup shaved parmesan cheese

for the dip

1/4 lemon juice

1/4 cup sour cream

1/4 cup mayonnaise

1/2 teaspoon dip mix & ranch dressing

1 teaspoon chipotle paste

Instructions

1. Using a medium sized mixing bowl, add in all the dip ingredients and incorporate together then refrigerate until ready to use.

2. Using a separate mixing bowl, add in the parmesan cheese, pork panko, salt then incorporate together and set aside.

3. Break the egg into a small bowl and whisk then dredge the diced beef steak in the egg mixture then the pork panko mix and transfer unto a paper lined plate.

4. Transfer the plate into a freezer and allow to set for 30 minutes then spray the fryer basket with cooking oil spray.

5. Heat the fryer up to 325°F then fry the steak nuggets for 3-5 minutes until browned.

6. Season the fried nuggets with little salt then serve along with the dip and enjoy as desired.

Nutrition Information

Calories: 350kcal | Carbohydrates: 1g | Protein: 40g | Fat: 20g

Egg & Bacon Slicone Cups

Preparation Time: 10 minutes

Cook Time: 15 minutes

Servings: 8

Ingredients

1/4 cup minced onions

1/4 cup diced red peppers

1/4 cup diced green peppers

1/4 cup chopped fresh spinach

1/4 cup shaved mozzarella cheese

1/2 cup shaved cheddar cheese

2 tablespoons heavy whipping cream

3 crumbled & cooked bacon slices

6 large eggs

salt & pepper, to taste

Instructions

1. Break the eggs into a large mixing bowl then add in the pepper, salt, whipping cream and whisk together until combined.

2. Add in the cheeses, onions, red peppers, spinach, green peppers, bacon and whisk together until incorporated.

3. Pour the mixture into 8 silicone molds and sprinkle the top with the remaining veggies then place the molds in the air fryer.

4. Cook at 300°F for 15 minutes then check to confirm if the eggs have set and done as desired.

5. Serve warm and enjoy as desired.

Nutrition Information

Calories: 156kcal | Carbohydrates: 3.1g | Protein: 10.5 g | Fat: 11.6g

Simple Fryer Bacon Slices

Preparation Time: 2 minutes

Cook Time: 10 minutes

Servings: 2

Ingredients

6 bacon slices

Instructions

1. Prepare the basket with a parchment paper then add in the bacon slices.

2. Air fryer at 380°F for 10 minutes then open and check for desired doneness.

3. Once done and ready, serve and enjoy with any dipping sauce of choice.

Nutrition Information

Calories: 120kcal | Carbohydrates: 0g | Protein: 7.5 | Fat: 10.5g

Ground Kheema Meat Loaf

Preparation Time: 10 minutes

Cook Time: 18 minutes

Servings: 4

Ingredients

1/8 teaspoon ground cardamom

1/4 cup chopped cilantro

1/2 teaspoon ground cinnamon

1 cup diced onion

1 teaspoon turmeric

1-pound lean ground beef

1 tablespoon minced ginger

1 tablespoon minced garlic

2 large eggs

2 teaspoons garam masala

salt & cayenne pepper to taste

Instructions

1. Using a large mixing bowl, add in all the ingredients and mix together until incorporated.

2. Transfer the meat batter into the fryer basket then air fry for 15 minutes at 360°F.

3. Slice the fried meat loaf, serve and enjoy as desired.

Nutrition Information

Calories: 260kcal | Carbohydrates: 6g | Protein: 26g | Fat: 13g

Creamy Taco Seasoned Meatballs

Preparation Time: 10 minutes

Cook Time: 15 minutes

Servings: 4

Ingredients

1/4 cup diced onions

1/4 cup chopped cilantro

1/2 cup shredded cheese

1 large eggs

1-pound lean ground beef

1 tablespoon minced garlic

2 tablespoons taco seasoning

kosher salt & black pepper, to taste

for the sauce

1/4 cup heavy cream

1/2 cup salsa

hot sauce

Instructions

1. Add all the ingredients into a mixing bowl then incorporate together until a paste like texture is achieved.

2. Scoop bits from the mixture and mold out 15 even sized meatballs.

3. Arrange the meatballs in the fryer basket then air fry for 10 minutes at 400°F.

4. In the meantime, combine all the sauce ingredients together.

5. Serve the meatballs and enjoy along with the creamy sauce.

Nutrition Information

Calories: 323kcal | Carbohydrates: 5g | Protein: 33g | Fat: 18g

Sirloin Steak Bulgogi

Preparation Time: 10 minutes

Cook Time: 12 minutes

Servings: 6

Ingredients

1/2 teaspoon ground black pepper

1 cup diced carrots

1 1/2 pounds sliced sirloin steak

2 tablespoons coconut oil

2 tablespoons brown sugar

2 tablespoons sesame seeds

2 teaspoons minced garlic cloves

3 tablespoons soy sauce

3 chopped green scallions

Instructions

1. Using a large ziploc bag, add in the green onions, carrots and sirloin steak.

2. Pour in the ground pepper, garlic, sesame seeds, coconut oil, brown sugar, soy sauce and massage into the steak.

3. Set the Ziploc bag aside to marinate for an hour.

4. Transfer the veggies and marinated beef into the fryer basket then air fry for 6 minutes at 400°F

5. Shale the fry basket and flip the beef over then air fry for an extra 6 minutes.

6. Serve and enjoy as desired.

Nutrition Information

Calories: 243kcal | Carbohydrates: 8g | Protein: 27g | Fat: 11g

Bun Thit Nuong

Preparation Time: 40 minutes

Cook Time: 10 minutes

Servings: 4

Ingredients

for the pork

1/4 cup diced onions

1/2 teaspoon black pepper

1 tablespoon fish sauce

1 tablespoon minced garlic cloves

1 pound pork shoulder, sliced thin

1 tablespoon minced lemongrass paste

2 tablespoons sugar

2 teaspoons soy sauce

2 tablespoons avocado oil

to garnish

1/4 cup crushed roasted peanuts

2 tablespoons cilantro, chopped

Instructions

1. Using a large mixing bowl, add in the black pepper, sugar, onions, avocado oil, soy sauce, fish sauce, garlic and lemongrass then combine together.

2. Cut the sliced pork shoulders crisscross ways into 4" pieces then add into the marinade and allow to marinate for 2 hours.

3. Transfer the marinated pork into the fryer basket then cook for 5 minutes at 400°F.

4. Flip the pork shoulders over and cook for an extra 5 minutes then transfer into serving platters.

5. Top with the cilantro, roasted peanuts, serve and enjoy as desired.

Nutrition Information

Calories: 231kcal | Carbohydrates: 4g | Protein: 16g | Fat: 16g

Easy, Air Fryer Italian Herb Pork Loin

Preparation Time: 5 minutes

Cook Time: 40 minutes

Servings: 8

Ingredients

1/4 cup Italian vinaigrette

1/2 teaspoon Italian Seasoning

1 teaspoon thyme

1 teaspoon rosemary

4 minced garlic cloves

4-pound boneless pork loin

salt & pepper, to taste

Instructions

1. Generously coat the pork loin with the Italian vinaigrette then sprinkle with the remaining seasoning.

2. Transfer the seasoned pork loin into a ziploc bag and place in a refrigerator for 2 hours to marinate.

3. Transfer the marinated pork loin into the fryer basket lined with parchment paper.

4. Air fry the pork loin at 360°F for 25 minutes.

5. Open the fryer and flip the pork over then fry for an extra 15 minutes.

6. Allow the pork to cool off then slices into pieces, glaze with extra vinaigrette, serve and enjoy as desired.

Nutrition Information

Calories: 125kcal | Carbohydrates: 1.1g | Protein: 9.1g | Fat: 8.8g

Juicy BBY Baby Ribs

Preparation Time: 30 minutes

Cook Time: 30 minutes

Servings: 4

Ingredients

1/2 cup bbq sauce

1 baby back rack ribs

1 tablespoon liquid smoke

3 tablespoons pork rub

salt & pepper, to taste

Instructions

1. Take the membrane off from the ribs back then slice the rib in half.

2. Drizzle the two sides of the rib with the liquid smoke then generously season with salt, pepper and pork rub.

3. Set the ribs aside to marinate for an hour then transfer into the fryer basket.

4. Air fry at 360°F for 15 minutes then flip over and fry for an extra 15 minutes.

5. Allow the ribs to cool for a few minutes then top with the sauce, serve and enjoy.

Nutrition Information

Calories: 88kcal | Carbohydrates: 19.8g | Protein: 0.3g | Fat: 0.4g

German Fryer Rouladen

Preparation Time: 10 minutes

Cook Time: 18 minutes

Servings: 4

Ingredients

for the sauce

1/4 cup chopped dill pickles

1/2 cup sour cream

1 tablespoon tomato paste

1 teaspoon chopped parsley

2 cups diced onion

3 tablespoons avocado oil

salt & pepper, to taste

for the meat

1/4 cup dijon mustard

1/4 cup chopped parsley

1-pound flank steak

1 teaspoon ground black pepper

4 bacon slices

Instructions

1. Using a small mixing bowl, add in the pepper, salt, diced onions and incorporate together.

2. Air fryer the seasoned onions for 6 minutes at 400°F.

3. Once fried, combine half of the onion with the chopped parsley, pickles, tomato paste, sour cream and add in a tablespoon of water you desire to thin out the sauce.

4. Cover the meat with the mustard then add on the slices of bacon, chopped parsley remaining fried onion and season with the pepper.

5. Tightly roll up the steak, holding it firm at the end then transfer into a slightly coated fryer basket.

6. Air fry the meat wrap for 10 minutes at 400°F, flipping the wrap halfway through cook time.

7. Serve and enjoy with the sauce mixture.

Nutrition Information

Calories: 443kcal | Carbohydrates: 10g | Protein: 29g | Fat: 31g

Spicy Fryer Bacon Pieces

Preparation Time: 5 minutes

Cook Time: 10 minutes

Servings: 3

Ingredients

1/4 cup hot sauce

1/2 cup pork rinds, crushed

6 uncooked bacon strips

Instructions

1. Slice the bacon strips into 6 pieces then transfer into a mixing bowl.

2. Pour the hot sauce into the mixing bowl and ensure the bacon pieces are well coated.

3. Dredge the coated bacon pieces in the crushed pork rinds until well covered.

4. Transfer the covered pieces into the fryer basket then air fry for 10 minutes at 350°F.

5. Serve and enjoy as desired.

Nutrition Information

Calories: 120.7kcal | Carbohydrates: 0g | Protein: 7.3g | Fat: 8.7g

SEAFOOD RECIPES

Fried Cheese Shrimp

Preparation Time: 7 minutes

Cook Time: 10 minutes

Servings: 4

Ingredients

1/2 teaspoon oregano

2/3 cup shaved parmesan cheese

1 teaspoon basil

1 teaspoon pepper

1 teaspoon powdered onion

2 tablespoons sesame oil

2 pounds peeled & deveined jumbo cooked shrimp

4 minced garlic cloves

quartered lime

Instructions

1. Using a large mixing bowl, add in the oil, powdered onion, basil, oregano, pepper, parmesan cheese, garlic and combine everything together.

2. Add the cooked shrimp into the mixture and toss together until well coated.

3. Grease the fryer basket with cooking spray oil then add in the coated shrimp then air fry for 10 minutes at 350°F.

4. Serve with a garnish of the lime juice and enjoy as desired.

Nutrition Information

Calories: 65kcal | Carbohydrates: 4.5g | Protein: 4.2g | Fat: 3.4g

Juicy Shrimp Scampi

Preparation Time: 5 minutes

Cook Time: 8 minutes

Servings: 4

Ingredients

1-pound raw shrimp

1 tablespoon juiced lime

1 tablespoon minced garlic

1 tablespoon chopped chives

1 tablespoon fresh chopped basil

2 tablespoons chicken stock

2 teaspoons red pepper flakes

4 tablespoons melted butter

Instructions

1. Add the pepper flakes, garlic and melted butter into the fryer basket then air fry until the butter, garlic and pepper are all incorporated for a minute.

2. Add in the remaining ingredients into the fryer basket then mix together.

3. Air fry the shrimp for 7 minutes at 390°F.

4. Serve, garnished with extra herbs if desired and enjoy.

Nutrition Information

Calories: 221kcal | Carbohydrates: 1g | Protein: 23g | Fat: 13g

Vegetable Glazed Salmon Fillets

Preparation Time: 20 minutes

Cook Time: 12 minutes

Servings: 2

Ingredients

1/4 cup soy sauce

1/2 teaspoon kosher salt

1/2 cup fresh juiced orange

1 tablespoon avocado oil

1 tablespoon chopped ginger

2 minced garlic cloves

2 (5 ounces) salmon fillets

2 teaspoons grated orange zest

3 tablespoons rice vinegar

for the veggies

1/2 teaspoon toasted sesame seeds

1 tablespoon sesame oil

2 ounces stemmed dry shiitake mushrooms

2 vertically halved heads baby bok choy

kosher salt, to taste

Instructions

1. Using a small mixing bowl, add in the avocado oil, soy sauce, salt, vinegar, orange juice, zest, ginger, garlic and whisk together until mixed.

2. Divide the marinade into 2 and reserve one then add the salmon fillets into a ziploc bag and pour the remaining soy sauce mix in to marinate for an hour.

3. Transfer the marinated salmon into the fryer basket then air fry for 6 minutes at 400°F.

4. In the meantime, coat the mushroom and bok choy with the oil, season with the salt then set aside.

5. Add the vegetables into the fryer basket along with the salmon fillets and fry for an extra 6 minutes.

6. Serve, drizzled with the reserved marinade, a garnish of the sesame seeds and enjoy.

Nutrition Information

Calories: 195kcal | Carbohydrates: 12g | Protein: 4g | Fat: 14g

Miso Coated Fryer Fillets

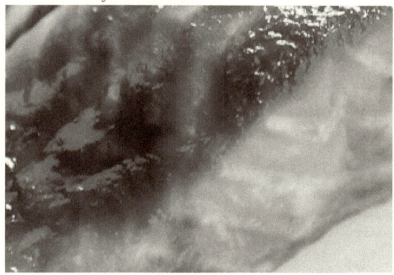

Preparation Time: 10 minutes

Cook Time: 10 minutes

Servings: 2

Ingredients

1/2 cup boiling water

1/2 teaspoon cracked black pepper

1 teaspoon diced ginger

1 teaspoon sesame seeds

1 teaspoons minced garlic cloves

2 tablespoons soy sauce

2 tablespoons white miso

2 chopped green scallions

2 tablespoons brown sugar

2 (5 ounces) salmon fillets

non-stick cooking spray

Instructions

1. Using a small mixing bowl, add in the pepper, ginger, garlic, miso, brown sugar, soy sauce and boiling water then combine together.

2. Using a flat work station, place the salmon fillets then cover with the sauce mixture, ensuring even amount of coating all over.

3. Grease the fryer basket with oil then add in the coated fillets and air fry for 12 minutes at 400°F

4. Serve with a garnish of scallions, sesame seeds and enjoy as desired.

Nutrition Information

Calories: 59kcal | Carbohydrates: 7g | Protein: 5g | Fat: 2g

Air Fried Creamy Scallops

Preparation Time: 5 minutes

Cook Time: 10 minutes

Servings: 2

Ingredients

1/2 teaspoon kosher salt

1/2 teaspoon ground black pepper

3/4 cup heavy whipping cream

1 teaspoon coconut oil

1 teaspoon minced garlic

1 tablespoon tomato paste

1 tablespoon chopped fresh basil

8 jumbo sea scallops

12 ounces' pack frozen spinach, drained & thawed

nonstick cooking oil spray

salt & pepper, to taste

Instructions

1. Grease the fryer basket then add in the drained & thawed spinach and keep to the side.

2. Generously season the scallops all over with oil, a sprinkle of salt & pepper then place inside the pan on the spinach.

3. Using a small mixing bowl, add in the extra pepper, salt, basil, tomato paste, garlic, heavy cream and mix together.

4. Then pour the cream mixture over the scallops and place in the air fryer.

5. Air fry the scallops for 10 minutes at 350°F then serve and enjoy as desired.

Nutrition Information

Calories: 359kcal | Carbohydrates: 6g | Protein: 9g | Fat: 33g

Simple Delicious Fryer Fillets

Preparation Time: 5 minutes

Cook Time: 12 minutes

Servings: 4

Ingredients

1/2 lime juice

1/2 lime wedges

1 tablespoon coconut oil

1 teaspoon powdered garlic

1 pound diced salmon fillets

2 teaspoons seafood seasoning

2 teaspoons lime pepper seasoning

salt, to taste

Instructions

1. Ensure the salmon fillets are completely dry then combine the lime juice and coconut oil together.

2. Thoroughly coat the dry salmon with the oil mixture then sprinkle with the salt and remaining seasonings.

3. Prepare the fryer basket with parchment paper then place in the salmon fillets and air fry at 360°F for 12 minutes.

4. Allow the fillets to cool off for a bit then serve, garnished with the lime wedges and enjoy.

Nutrition Information

Calories: 238kcal | Carbohydrates: 1g | Protein: 28.8g | Fat: 12.6g

Vegetable Salmon Cakes

Preparation Time: 35 minutes

Cook Time: 15 minutes

Servings: 5

Ingredients

1/4 cup mashed avocado

1/4 cup chopped cilantro, with extra

1/4 cup tapioca starch, with 4 extra teaspoons

1/2 teaspoon salt

1/2 cup coconut flakes

1-pound salmon

1 1/2 teaspoon yellow curry powder

2 large eggs

avocado oil

for the greens

1/2 teaspoon salt

2 teaspoons olive oil

6 cups arugula & spinach mix

Instructions

1. Skin the salmon then chop into pieces and transfer into a large mixing bowl.

2. Add in the cilantro, salt, curry powder, avocado and incorporate together.

3. Pour in the teaspoons of tapioca then mix together until combined then mold the patties into 10 even sizes.

4. Transfer the molded patties into a parchment paper prepared baking sheet then freeze for about 30 minutes.

5. In the meantime, whisk the eggs together in a mixing bowl and pour the coconut flakes, 1/4 cup of tapioca into different bowls.

6. Coat the fryer basket with oil then heat up to 400°F for 10 minutes.

7. Run the chilled patties through the tapioca until coated, then dredge in the egg mix and finally coat with the coconut flakes.

8. Transfer the covered patties into the preheated fryer then fry for 15 minutes until the crispy and tenderized.

9. Using a large pan, heat the olive oil up over medium heat then add in the spinach, arugula, salt and stir cook for a minute until wilted.

10. Serve the salmon cakes and greens together, enjoying with a garnish of cilantro.

Nutrition Information

Calories: 572kcal | Carbohydrates: 41.3g | Protein: 27.9g | Fat: 36.6g

VEGETABLE RECIPES

Fryer Roasted Asian Broccoli Florets

Preparation Time: 10 minutes

Cook Time: 20 minutes

Servings: 4

Ingredients

1/8 teaspoon kosher salt

1/3 cup roasted peanuts, salted

1 teaspoon rice vinegar

1-pound broccoli florets

1 tablespoon minced garlic

1 1/2 tablespoons olive oil

2 teaspoons honey

2 teaspoons sriracha

2 tablespoon low-salt soy sauce

juiced lemon, if desired

Instructions

1. Using a large mixing bowl, add in the garlic, olive oil, sea salt, broccoli florets and incorporate together until well coated.

2. Arrange the coated broccoli florets in a single layer in the fryer basket, ensuring enough space as possible.

3. Cook for 20 minutes at 400°F until golden brown and crispy.

Note: Stir together after 10 minutes of cook time.

4. In the meantime, combine the rice vinegar, honey, sriracha and soy sauce together using a microwave safe bowl.

5. Once combined microwave the mixture for 15 seconds until mixed and the honey is melted.

6. Serve the prepared broccoli then coat with the vinegar mixture and toss together.

7. Add in the roasted peanuts and stir then top with the juiced lemon.

8. Serve and enjoy as desired.

Nutrition Information

Calories: 187kcal | Carbohydrates: 8.9g | Protein: 4.7g | Fat: 12.4g

Herbal Brussels Sprouts

Preparation Time: 10 minutes

Cook Time: 8 minutes

Servings: 4

Ingredients

1/4 teaspoon salt

1/2 teaspoon dried thyme

1 pound brussels sprouts

1 teaspoon parsley, dried

1 teaspoon powdered garlic

2 teaspoon sesame oil

Instructions

1. Using a large mixing bowl, add all the ingredients in and toss together until the brussels are well coated.

2. Empty the bowl contents into the fryer basket then roast for 8 minutes at 390°F

3. Once done, allow to cool for a bit then serve and enjoy as desired.

Nutrition Information

Calories 79kcal | Carbohydrates: 12g | Protein: 4g | Fat: 2g

Cauliflower Potato Patties

Preparation Time: 15minutes

Cook Time: 20 minutes

Servings: 10

Ingredients

1/4 teaspoon cumin

1/4 cup sunflower seeds

1/4 cup ground flaxseed

1/2 teaspoon chili powder

1 minced green onion

1 cup packed cilantro

1 peeled large sweet potato

1 teaspoon minced garlic cloves

2 cup cauliflower florets

2 tablespoons ranch seasoning mix

2 tablespoons plain gluten free flour

any dipping sauce

salt & pepper, to taste

Instructions

1. Dice the peeled potatoes into small chunks then process in a blender until chopped into smaller pieces.

2. Add the minced onion and cauliflower florets into the blender and pulse together again.

3. Add in the cilantro, plain flour, flaxseed, sunflower seeds and remaining seasonings then pulse together until a thick batter is achieved.

4. Transfer the batter out of the blender then use 1/4 cup of the batter to mold 1 1/2" thick patties then transfer in the freezer to set.

5. Once ready place the patties in the air fryer and fry for 18-20 minutes at 360°F.

6. Once done, serve and enjoy as desired.

Nutrition Information

Calories: 85kcal | Carbohydrates: 9g | Protein: 2.7g | Fat: 2.9g

Tofu Fried Cauliflower Rice

Preparation Time: 10 minutes

Cook Time: 20 minutes

Servings: 3

Ingredients

for the tofu

1/2 block firm tofu

1/2 cup chopped onion

1 teaspoon turmeric

1 cup chopped carrot

2 tablespoons low salt soy sauce

for the cauliflower

1/2 cup frozen peas

1/2 cup chopped broccoli

1 tablespoon rice vinegar

1 tablespoon ginger, minced

1 1/2 teaspoons sesame oil, toasted

2 minced garlic cloves

2 tablespoons low salt soy sauce

3 cups riced cauliflower

Instructions

1. Using a large mixing bowl, add in the tofu and crumble then pour in the remaining ingredients for the tofu and incorporate together.

2. Transfer the coated tofu into the fryer basket then fry for 10 minutes at 370°F.

3. In the meantime, add all the cauliflower ingredients together and incorporate until mixed the transfer into the fryer basket after the 10 minutes of initial cooking.

4. Shake the fryer basket together then continue to fry for an extra 10 minutes, shaking just once mid cook time.

5. Check for desired doneness and add an extra 2- minutes of cook time if required.

6. Serve and enjoy as desired.

Nutrition Information

Calories: 263kcal | Carbohydrates: 28.3g | Protein: 13g | Fat: 6g

Cheese Filled Mushrooms

Preparation Time: 7 minutes

Cook Time: 8 minutes

Servings: 5

Ingredients

1/8 cup shaved white cheddar cheese

1/8 cup shaved sharp cheddar cheese

1/4 cup shaved parmesan cheese

1 teaspoon Worcestershire sauce

2 minced garlic cloves

4 ounces cream cheese

8 ounces mushrooms

salt & pepper, to taste

Instructions

1. Chop the mushroom stem off then soften cream cheese in a microwave for about 15 seconds.

2. Using a medium mixing bowl, add in the Worcestershire sauce, pepper, salt, cream cheese, cheddar cheeses and combine together.

3. Stuff the stemmed mushrooms with the cheese mixture and transfer into the fryer basket.

4. Fry the mushrooms at 370°F for 8 minutes then allow to cool before serving and enjoying as desired.

Nutrition Information

Calories: 195kcal | Carbohydrates: 5.4g | Protein: 5.8g | Fat: 18.3g

Parmesan Cheese Kale Chip

Preparation Time: 5 minutes

Cook Time: 10 minutes

Servings: 12

Ingredients

1/4 cup shredded parmesan cheese

1 tablespoon avocado oil

10 ounces chopped kale, ribs removed

salt & pepper, to taste

Instructions

1. Using a large mixing bowl, add in the kale and coat with the salt, pepper and avocado oil.

2. Transfer the coated kale into the fryer basket the air fry for 5 minutes at 270°F.

3. Open the fryer and shake the basket then cook for an extra 3 minutes.

4. Open the fryer again and sprinkle with the shredded parmesan cheese and cook for an extra 2 minutes.

5. Serve warm and enjoy as desired.

Nutrition Information

Calories: 30kcal | Carbohydrates: 2.4g | Protein: 1.6g | Fat: 1.9g

Lime Drizzled Asparagus

Preparation Time: 5 minutes

Cook Time: 10 minutes

Servings: 4

Ingredients

1 bunch fresh asparagus

1 1/2 teaspoons Herbes de Provence

lime wedge

cooking spray oil

salt & pepper, to taste

Instructions

1. Trim the asparagus hard ends off and wash then pat dry.

2. Drizzle the asparagus with the spray oil and coat with the seasonings.

3. Transfer the asparagus into the fryer basket then cook until crisp for 10 minutes at 360°F.

4. Serve, drizzled with the lime juice then enjoy as desired.

Nutrition Information

Calories: 382kcal | Carbohydrates: 62.6g | Protein: 62.5g | Fat: 0.6g

Crispy Vinegar Onion Sprouts

Preparation Time: 10 minutes

Cook Time: 10 minutes

Servings: 5

Ingredients

1/2 cup diced red onions

1 tablespoon balsamic vinegar

2 cups halved fresh brussels sprouts

cooking oil spray

salt & pepper, to taste

Instructions

1. Add the brussels and onions into a medium sized mixing bowl then drizzle with the vinegar and cooking spray.

2. Season the coated sprouts with salt & pepper, massaging the seasoning in.

3. Coat the fryer basket with the remaining spray then add in the seasoned brussels and onions.

4. Air fry at 350°F for 5 minutes then toss the onion and brussel together and cook until crisp for an extra 5 minutes.

5. Allow the sprouts to cool off a bit then serve and enjoy as desired.

Nutrition Information

Calories: 26kcal | Carbohydrates: 3.4g | Protein: 1.4g | Fat: 0.6g

Cheesy Cream Spinach

Preparation Time: 10 minutes

Cook Time: 15 minutes

Servings: 2

Ingredients

1/4 cup parmesan cheese, shredded

1/2 cup diced onions

1/2 teaspoon ground nutmeg

1 teaspoon kosher salt

1 teaspoon ground black pepper

2 teaspoons minced garlic

4 ounces shaved cream cheese

10-ounce pack thawed frozen spinach

Instructions

1. Using a medium mixing bowl, add in the shaved cream cheese, spinach, garlic, onion, nutmeg, salt & pepper then combine together.

2. Transfer the cream mixture into the greased fryer basket then air fry for 10 minutes at 350°F.

3. Open the air fryer and stir the mixture together again then top with the parmesan cheese.

4. Air fry again until the cheese is browned and melted for 5 minutes at 400°F.

5. Serve and enjoy as desired.

Nutrition Information

Calories: 273kcal | Carbohydrates: 8g | Protein: 8g | Fat: 23g

Air Fried Pearl Onions

Preparation Time: 5 minutes

Cook Time: 20 minutes

Servings: 3

Ingredients

2 tablespoons avocado oil

2 tablespoons balsamic vinegar

2 teaspoons chopped fresh rosemary

15 ounces frozen pearl onions

kosher salt & black pepper, to taste

Instructions

1. Using a medium mixing bowl, add in the onions, rosemary, pepper, oli, salt, vinegar and toss around until combined.

2. Transfer the coated pearl onions into the fryer basket then air fry for 20 minutes at 400°F.

3. Serve and enjoy as desired.

Nutrition Information

Calories: 92kcal | Carbohydrates: 2g | Fat: 9g

Green Beans & Bacon Slices

Preparation Time: 15 minutes

Cook Time: 10 minutes

Servings: 4

Ingredients

3 cups frozen cut green beans

3 bacon slices

1/4 cup water

kosher salt & black pepper, to taste

Instructions

1. Using a small heatproof pan. add in the water, bacon slices, onion and green beans.

2. Place the pan into the fryer basket then air fry for 15 minutes at 375°F.

3. Increase the temperature to 400°F for another 5 minutes.

4. Season with the salt, pepper and mix together.

5. Serve and enjoy as desired.

Nutrition Information

Calories: 95kcal | Carbohydrates: 6g | Protein: 3g | Fat: 6g

Air Fried Vegetables

Preparation Time: 5 minutes

Cook Time: 23 minutes

Servings: 4

Ingredients

2 cups diced radishes

1 cup diced onion

1 cup diced bell peppers

2 tablespoons melted butter

5 minced garlic cloves

kosher salt & black pepper, to taste

Instructions

1. Using a large mixing bowl add in the pepper, salt, garlic, bell peppers, onions, radishes and combine together.

2. Cover the vegetable mixture with the melted butter and incorporate then transfer into the fryer basket.

3. Air fry the veggies for 20 minutes at 360 F and cook for extra minutes if you want a crispier texture.'

4. Serve and enjoy as desired.

Nutrition Information

Calories: 88kcal | Carbohydrates: 9g | Protein: 1g | Fat: 6g

DESSERTS & APPETIZERS RECIPES

Creamy Bacon Stuffed Jalapeno

Preparation Time: 10 minutes

Cook Time: 5 minutes

Servings: 5

Ingredients

1/4 cup cheddar cheese, shredded

2 chopped & cooked bacon slices

6 ounces cream cheese, softened

10 fresh jalapenos

cooking oil spray

Instructions

1. Vertically half the jalapenos and remove the seeds.

2. Add the bacon slices, cream cheese and cheddar cheese into a mixing bowl then combine together.

3. Fill of the seeded jalapeno slices with the cheese mixture.

4. Coat the fryer basket with the cooking oil and add in the stuffed jalapenos

5. Cook for 5 minutes at 370°F then allow to cool before enjoying as desired.

Nutrition Information

Calories: 274kcal | Carbohydrates: 26.1g | Protein: 8.6g | Fat: 19.8g

Simple Cream Cheesecake

Preparation Time: 7 minutes

Cook Time: 2 minutes

Servings: 2

Ingredients

1/2 cup erythritol

1/2 cup almond flour

1/2 teaspoon vanilla extract

2 tablespoons erythritol

4 tablespoons divided heavy cream

8 ounces cream cheese

Instructions

1. Allow the cream cheese to soften then incorporate with the 2 tablespoons heavy cream, vanilla, and 1/2 cup erythritol until smooth and combined.

2. Transfer the mixture onto a baking sheet lined with parchment paper then place in the freezer until firm.

3. Using a medium sized bowl, add in the almond flour and tablespoons erythritol then mix together.

4. Dip the cheesecake bites into the remaining heavy cream then run through the flour mixture.

5. Arrange the bites into the fryer basket and air fry for 2 minutes at 300°F.

6. Serve and enjoy as desired.

Nutrition Information

Calories: 540kcal | Carbohydrates: 8.7g | Protein: 8.5g | Fat: 52.6g

Cheese Filled Jalapeno Poppers

Preparation Time: 10 minutes

Cook Time: 7 minutes

Servings: 5

Ingredients

1 diced onion

1 minced garlic clove

4 ounces goat cheese

5 medium jalapenos

salt, to taste

powdered chili

crushed red pepper

a handful of cilantro

Instructions

1. Deseed the jalapenos then half each one of them.

2. Combine the onion, garlic, cilantro, red pepper, chili, salt and goat cheese together.

3. Spoon the cheese mixture into the halved jalapenos and arrange in the fryer basket.

4. Air fry for 7 minutes at 350°F.

5. Serve and enjoy as desired.

Nutrition Information

Calories: 263kcal | Carbohydrates: 30.1g | Protein: 4.8g | Fat: 5g

Bulgogi Hamburgers

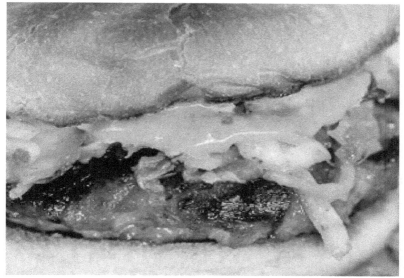

Preparation Time: 15 minutes

Cook Time: 10 minutes

Servings: 4

Ingredients

for the burgers

1/4 cup chopped green scallions

1/2 teaspoon salt

1 tablespoon soy sauce

1 tablespoon sesame oil

1-pound Lean ground beef

2 teaspoon sugar

2 tablespoon gochujang

2 teaspoon minced ginger

2 teaspoon minced garlic

for the mayonnaise

1/4 cup mayonnaise

1/4 cup chopped green scallions

1 tablespoon gochujang

1 tablespoon coconut oil

2 teaspoon sesame seeds

4 hamburger buns, to serve

Instructions

1. Using a large mixing bowl, add in onions, sugar, oil, ginger, garlic, soy sauce, gochujang, salt and ground beef then incorporate together.

2. Allow the beef to marinate for an hour then mold into four different patties.

3. Place the patties into the fryer basket then air fry for 10 minutes at 360°F.

4. In the meantime, combine the scallions, sesame seeds, oil, gochujang and mayonnaise together.

5. Serve the burger along with the mayonnaise mixture and enjoy as desired.

Nutrition Information

Calories: 392kcal | Carbohydrates: 7g | Protein: 24g | Fat: 29g

Montreal Beef Burgers

Preparation Time: 10 minutes

Cook Time: 10 minutes

Servings: 4

Ingredients

for the seasoning

1 teaspoon cumin seeds

1 teaspoon kosher salt

1 teaspoon dried garlic

1 teaspoon coriander seeds

1 teaspoon black mustard seeds

1 teaspoon dried red pepper flakes

2 teaspoons whole black peppercorns

for the beef

1-pound ground beef

2 tablespoons Worcestershire sauce

4 large lettuce leaves

Instructions

1. Add the peppercorns, salt, pepper, garlic, coriander and cumin into a mixing bowl then combine until mixed and grounded.

2. Add in the beef, sauce and incorporate together then form into 4 different patties.

3. Transfer the molded patties into the fryer basket then air fry for 10 minutes at 350°F.

4. Serve using the lettuce leaves and enjoy as desired.

Nutrition Information

Calories: 182kcal | Carbohydrates: 5g | Protein: 25g | Fat: 6g

Simple Air Fryer Hard Boiled Eggs

Preparation Time:

Cook Time: 15 minutes

Servings: 6

Ingredients

6 large eggs

Instructions

1. Place the eggs in the fryer basket then fry at 260°F for 15 minutes.

2. Transfer the hard boiled eggs into cold water to cool off.

3. Break and peel the shells and enjoy as desired.

Nutrition Information

Calories: 70kcal | Carbohydrates: 0g | Protein: 6g | Fat: 5g

Quick Fryer Sausage

Preparation Time: 5

Cook Time: 20 minutes

Servings: 5

Ingredients

5 uncooked sausage links

Instructions

1. Prepare the fryer basket with parchment paper then add in the sausage.

2. Cook at 360°F for 15 minutes then flip the sausage over and cook for an extra 5 minutes.

3. Allow the sausage to cool off for a bit then serve and enjoy as desired.

Nutrition Information

Calories: 95kcal | Carbohydrates: 0.5g | Protein: 6g | Fat: 7g

Creamy Cheese Queso Fundido

Preparation Time: 10 minutes

Cook Time: 25 minutes

Servings: 4

Ingredients

1/2 cup half and half

1 cup diced tomatoes

1 cup chopped onions

1 tablespoon minced garlic

2 diced jalapenos

2 teaspoons ground cumin

2 cups shredded mozzarella cheese

4 ounces' chorizo with the casings removed

Instructions

1. Combine the cumin, jalapenos, garlic, onion, tomatoes and chorizo together.

2. Transfer the mixture into the fryer basket then air fry for 15 minutes at 400°F.

3. Add in the halt and half, cheese and stir together.

4. Air fry for 10 minutes at 320°F.

5. Serve and enjoy as desired.

Nutrition Information

Calories: 328kcal | Carbohydrates: 11g | Protein: 18g | Fat: 23g

Coconut Chicken Meatballs

Preparation Time: 10 minutes

Cook Time: 15 minutes

Servings: 4

Ingredients

1/4 cup unsweetened shredded coconut

1/2 cup chopped cilantro

1 tablespoon soy sauce

1 teaspoon avocado oil

1-pound ground chicken

1 tablespoon hoisin sauce

1 teaspoon sriracha sauce

2 chopped green scallions

salt & pepper, to taste

Instructions

1. Using a large mixing bowl, add in all the ingredients and combine together.

2. Scoop the batter into bits, mold meatballs out of the mixture and arrange in the fryer basket.

3. Air fry at 350°F for 5 minutes then flip the meatballs over and continue cook for another 5 minutes.

4. Serve and enjoy as desired.

Nutrition Information

Calories: 223kcal | Carbohydrates: 3g | Protein: 20g | Fat: 14g

Simple BBQ Meatballs

Preparation Time: 10 minutes

Cook Time: 15 minutes

Servings: 5

Ingredients

1/4 cup shredded cheddar cheese

1/2 cup bbq sauce

1/2 cup almond meal

1/2 cup diced onions

1 large egg

1 pound ground beef

1 teaspoon steak seasoning

1 teaspoon Worcestershire sauce

2 minced garlic cloves

salt & pepper, to taste

Instructions

1. Using a large mixing bowl, add in the Worcestershire sauce, cheddar cheese, egg, onions, almond meal, garlic, seasonings, ground beef and combine together until molded into 1.

2. Scoop the batter into bits and mold out 10 even meatballs then arrange on a parchment paper.

3. Transfer the meatballs loaded parchment paper into the fryer basket then air fry ar 365°F for 8 minutes.

4. Flip the meatballs over then air fry for an extra 7 minutes.

5. Serve hot and enjoy drizzled with the sauce.

Nutrition Information

Calories: 417kcal | Carbohydrates: 18.9g | Protein: 28g | Fat: 25.4g

END

Thank you for reading my book.

Jose White

Printed in the USA
CPSIA information can be obtained
at www.ICGtesting.com
LVHW092143101024
793543LV00034B/842